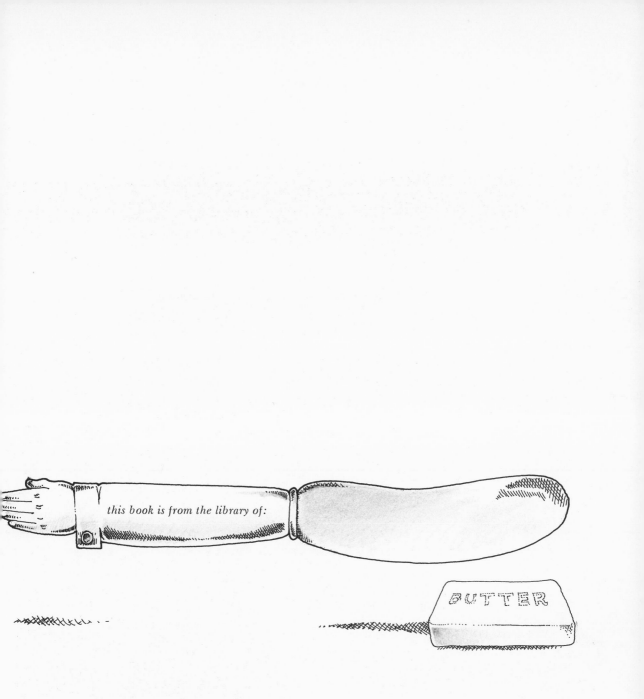

A SIMPLE BOOK ABOUT THE PLEASURES O

THE BAKERS

Scribners

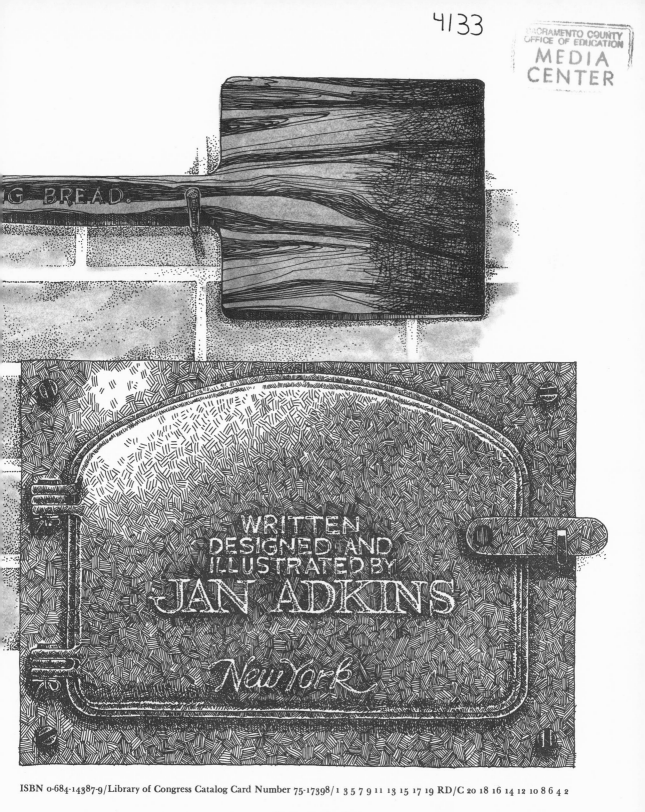

WRITTEN
DESIGNED AND
ILLUSTRATED BY
JAN ADKINS

New York

ISBN 0-684-14387-9/Library of Congress Catalog Card Number 75-17398/1 3 5 7 9 11 13 15 17 19 RD/C 20 18 16 14 12 10 8 6 4 2

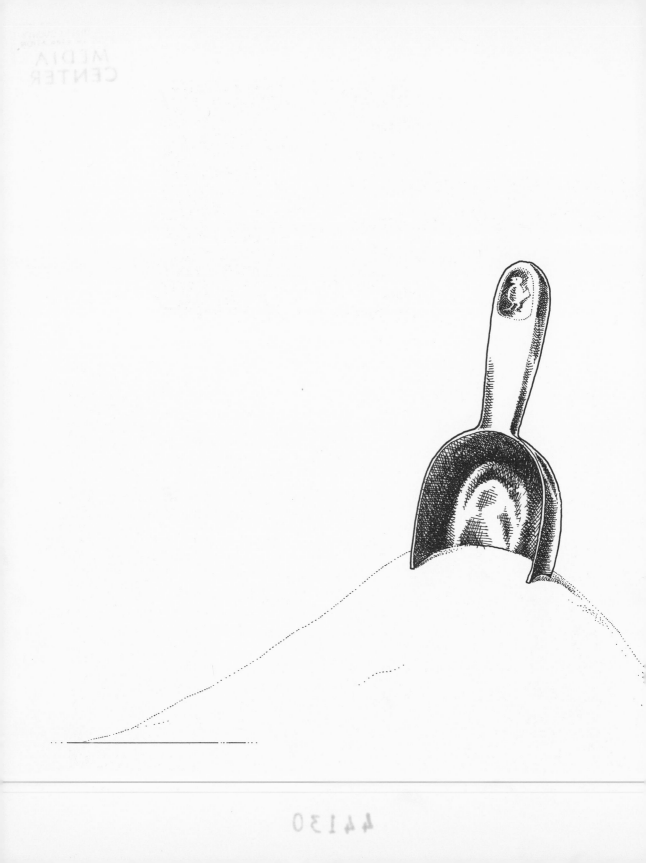

Sally sings the sun asleep, and sings so softly high,
Her song awakes the sleeping stars as they go slipping by.
The stars they turn and stir themselves at Sally's song to learn,
They flicker to their proper place, and all in chorus: Burn.

This book, and most of everything else,
is for Sally.

Further back than the time all stories are once upon . . . long, long ago when men and women were just meeting the world, they began to make bread. It was not bread you would recognize. They gathered wild grains and crushed them between stones, blew away some of the stems and hulls, mixed the grain with water and baked this grain-paste in the coals of their fire. Bread.

In Egypt, six thousand years ago, the first real bread was baked. The Great Valley of the Nile was rich with wheat, the best grain for bread. Foam from beermaking, full of yeast, was mixed with wheat dough and baked, and there were round, brown loaves of sweet-smelling bread, just as you might bake today or tomorrow morning. Six thousand years is not so long.

Greek heroes of the *Iliad,* and plain folks tending their olive trees and sheep, ate dark wheat loaves with olives and wine, lamb, and fish, but they also ate a kind of bread-paste. It was made from other kinds of grains—millet and barley —or from beans and lentils. A little oil and some spices were added and it was eaten with the fingers.

You could get a good loaf of bread in Rome. Around two thousand years ago Romans had bread of every kind (the city itself used fourteen million bushels of wheat every year): light bread, dark bread, sweet bread, salty bread, rolls, flatbreads, square breads, all kinds. Bakers ground the wheat shipped from Egypt and North Africa and baked it into large and small loaves. They sold them to be eaten dry, or dipped in water, wine, or goat's milk.

Europe in the ninth century was not a happy place. Wars, famines, and epidemics made great sadness. In good years nourishing bread and vegetables made up most of the diet. Rye grew with the wheat in these northern fields, and they were harvested together to make a light brown flour called *maslin*. At times, a dreadful fungus called *ergot* infected the rye, and folks who ate the infected bread went mad and died terribly. Sad times.

Bread was important in the Middle Ages; so important that a baker caught selling impure or underweight loaves was in serious trouble. Bread was most of the meal, and it was the dish, too: folks ate on pieces of stalish, unleavened bread called *trenchers,* about six inches by four inches, which sopped up the juices. After the meal the trenchers were given to the servants or the poor.

The first settlers to North America brought wheat for planting, but found a solid, deep forest reaching inland farther than settlements would go for three hundred years. The wheat grew poorly in the rocky, root-choked fields they cut out of the green wall before them, but the native Americans showed them how easily corn grew there, and how delicious corn flatbread could be.

Bread travelled. It travelled in the holds of ships as the rock-hard *ship's biscuit*, or *hardtack*. Sailors rapped them on the edges of their tables to knock the weevils out, and ate them with salt pork or bully beef. Trappers and pioneers carried breadmakings with them—some flour and a lump of yeasty dough. Many kept the yeast mixture warm in a small leather bag hung around their necks, and these people were called "sourdoughs" for the strong smell of the working yeast.

At the Vienna World's Fair in 1873, Governor Washburn of Minnesota ate "Viennese rolls" made from a very white flour developed by Hungarian millers. When he returned to the United States he brought Hungarian millers and their flour mills to process Minnesota wheat. The special porcelain rollers of the new flour mills broke up the parts of the wheat kernel that colored it, but also squeezed out the wheat germ that made bread so nutritious. The bread was whiter, but not as nourishing.

Millers and bakers—and later engineers and chemists—pursued "whiteness" in bread, assuming that whiter bread was purer. Without the wheat germ and its bit of oil, the flour would not spoil and could be kept for a long time, an advantage for the miller only. They milled their flour, sieved it, bleached it with harsh and dangerous chemicals, and added ridiculous white powders to make it bright—ash, alum, chalk, yech! The whiter it got, the less nutritious it became.

The bread shelf at the supermarket is long and as flashy as a banner-fluttering used-car lot. Hundreds of colorful plastic wrappers hold bread not much more nourishing and only a little tastier than medical cotton. The bread is very white; if a low germ-count per slice really is purity, then it is pure. The wrappers announce that their bread is "enriched," "vitamin-fortified," "body-building." Is it wonderfully healthy stuff?

The few vitamins factory bakers dribble back into the dead white flour are much less than what they've torn out, the bulk and roughage so good for digestion are left far behind, and the bleaches and nonspoilage additives are certainly not nourishing. The wholesomeness of the whole grain is seldom inside the supermarket wrappers.

For five thousand years, bread—fragrant, toothy food—has kept men and women satisfied and healthy. Would a slice or two of supermarket bread and a pot of beer keep a stonemason all afternoon? No. How far could a centurion march on a loaf of cotton bread and a string of onions? Not far. A thousand loaves of a spongy business someone wants you to think of as bread, and not one that's a meal for a hungry body.

You have three alternatives: you can cultivate a taste for the tasteless, for cotton bread; you can find a fine bakery, a good place for smells and tastes; or you can bring the smells and tastes into your own kitchen and cultivate a taste for fragrant, toothy food, for real bread.

Bread is simple. Simple to make, simple to bake, simple to eat. Why folks think it is difficult to bake bread is a mystery. Flour, water, yeast, a little oil, a bit of sugar, a pinch of salt—bread. Not only bread, but also a kitchen fragrant and warm, the smiles of satisfied bread-eaters, and the satisfaction of having mixed and kneaded and shaped a basic part of life with your own hands.

First the flour, the body of the bread. Wheat was found growing wild in Asia Minor thousands of years ago. It was harvested with flint sickles and the best grains were probably kept for seed when men and women learned to plant and tend and gather. The Egyptians held it sacred, and sent boxes of seed wheat, harvested with copper sickles, into the after-life with their pharaohs. Since then it has been harvested with bronze, iron, and steel sickles, with the first Mc-Cormick reaper, and with giant combines, but it has always been as important. There are other grains—corn, oats, rye, barley—but none has the character of wheat.

Wheat grows as a stalk with *wheat berries* at the tip. Before machine combines, the wheat was cut down with a scythe and bound into *sheaves* for carrying. They were taken to be *threshed,* emptied onto the *threshing floor,* and beaten with *flails* to separate the berries from the wheat stalks (which are used as hay). *Flailing* also loosened the *husks* and *beards* (these are called *chaff*) from the wheat berries. The wheat berries and the chaff were *winnowed,* or tossed into the air on a windy day; the lighter chaff was blown away and the heavier berries

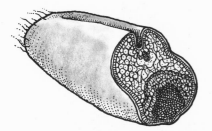

fell back down. The wheat was then taken to the miller. He owned a windmill or a watermill or a donkey-mill: considerable power was needed to turn the stone grinding-wheel on its brother wheel. The miller fed the grain between the two and it was ground fine. He often *bolted* the flour—sieved it through cloth to remove impurity or larger bits. Today all this happens inside machines, but if you look carefully you may be able, still, to get flour as good as it ever was.

There are two kinds of wheat flour, hard and soft. Hard flour is made from hard winter wheat and is best for bread, baking up into a firm, elastic loaf that takes some chewing. Soft wheat is sometimes seen as *pastry flour,* and gives a cakier, softer crumb. It can be used, but it is not the best choice. If you buy white flour, try to get *unbleached* white; it has a better texture and taste. White flour may be kept without refrigeration for some time, but keep it tightly sealed.

Whole wheat flour has the wheat germ ground in with it. It will not keep for a long time, but it tastes better, and is much better for you. *Whole meal* flour is coarser, with some bran, and *graham* flour is also coarse, with more bran. These light brown, speckled flours should be kept tightly sealed in the refrigerator.

There are other flours—from rye, corn, oats, barley, buckwheat, soybeans, rice—and someday you should experiment with them, but they haven't got what makes bread: gluten, an elastic material in wheat. Fool with them after you enjoy what wheat flour can teach you.

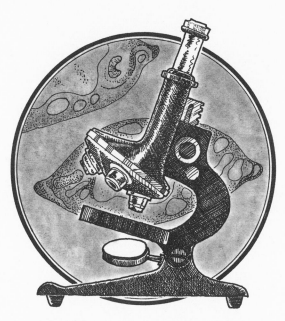

What makes bread? It is an elastic material (the gluten in wheat flour) expanded to a spongy mass. What makes the holes in the spongy mass? Gas expanding inside it. And what makes the gas? Yeast.

Yeast is a microscopic plant, *Saccharomyces cerivisae*, which is about 1/4000 as long as its name. It is a clever plant, because it takes apart sugars and starches to make, among other things, carbon dioxide gas. The gas makes bubbles in the dough, which expand during baking to make the holes.

Yeast comes in several forms: as a working yeast mixture, like the sourdoughs carried, which must be mixed with dough to rise several hours before use; as a soft, refrigerated cake which should be dissolved in lukewarm water and set to rest for five or ten minutes before it is used; easiest to use is powdered yeast, which is dissolved in lukewarm water and used immediately.

Take care of your yeast. Remember what it likes and what it doesn't like. Yeast likes sugar—it grows quickly with a little sugar to work on. Yeast likes warmth—100° to 110°, a little warmer than body temperature. Yeast doesn't like bright light or salt. You want to coddle it, help it grow fast, and then set it to work.

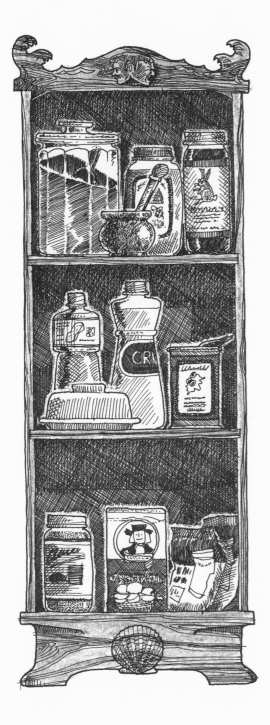

SUGAR Sugar is more than flavor. It encourages yeast to grow quickly in the dough. You can choose the flavor you want: granulated sugar or sugar syrup will work, but lack a flavor of their own; brown sugar is rich; honey has a flowery taste; and molasses has a dark, deep, very slightly bitter sweetness.

OIL Oil is one of the necessities. It makes bread tender and gives it a good crumb. There are several good oils and shortenings: butter, lard, vegetable oil, olive oil, corn oil, peanut oil, and others. Special oil can give bread a special flavor.

DRY MILK It adds nutrients, and gives the bread a moister, cakier texture that you may or may not want. Without dry milk, a bread is chewier.

WHEAT GERM This light brown powder is the germ taken out of white flour. It adds texture and a nutty flavor and a great deal of nourishment.

CORNMEAL Cornmeal is used for cornbread, but it is also sprinkled on baking sheets to prevent sticking and to give a solid bottom crust.

mixing bowl
mixing spoon
wire whisk
measuring cups
measuring spoons
timer
glazing brush
dough scraper
bread knife
cutting board

3 cups lukewarm water
2 packets yeast
¼ cup sweetening
4 cups flour

The only difficult part of making bread is deciding when to start. Any day will do, any time you have four hours together. I like Saturday, some like Thursday, but whatever day you pick to be Bread Day will become a favorite day. Make sure you have the time, because bread isn't to be rushed.

You will make a *sponge,* a runny flour and yeast and sweetening mixture. The sponge is a good environment for yeast, and after it has bubbled and frothed and expanded to about two times its original size, it will be full of active yeast ready to work on the rest of the dough.

The biggest bowl or pot or pan you can find is probably not too big. About eighteen inches across and twelve inches deep is about right. The sponge, and later the dough, are going to expand, and unless you want them all over the place, get a big bowl.

Sprinkle two packets of dry yeast onto three cups of water that feels only a little warm to your wrist. This recipe is for whole wheat flour; if you are using white flour, a little more than one packet will do. Mix in the yeast granules until they are dissolved, then add one-fourth cup of sweetening— I like half honey and half molasses, some like a little more than one-fourth cup to make the bread sweeter, and you can find out what you like.

Mix in four cups of flour, a cup at a time, and when it is all mixed, beat it (hard) 100 strokes. When you get to stroke 65, you will know why bakers have strong arms.

There is probably a warm place in your home, away from drafts and running people. If there isn't, turn your oven on low for a minute or so, turn it off, and put the bowl in the oven with a slightly damp dish towel across the top. Let the sponge *rise* (expand) for 60 minutes. Let it alone and let the yeast grow.

¼ cup oil
1¼ tablespoons salt
5 cups flour

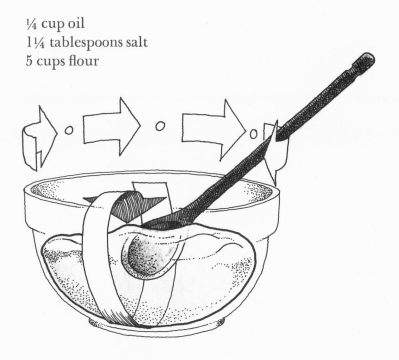

You can add the salt, now, which would have slowed down the yeast's growth. Sprinkle it on the sponge and dribble the oil over it, too. With a big, long-handled spoon, *fold* the salt and oil in. *Folding* is a way to mix ingredients without cutting through the sponge. Think of the sponge as a flabby ball; slide the spoon under it and fold it over on itself. Turn the bowl a little and do it again, over and over, turning the bowl.

Add the flour, folding it in a cup at a time. The dough will come unstuck from the bowl, but keep folding until it can't seem to take any more flour. Sprinkle some flour onto a clean table or counter—a surface about eighteen inches by twenty-four inches without cracks—and turn the dough out of the bowl onto it.

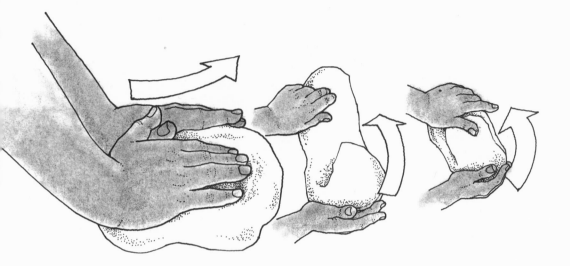

Kneading, you are stretching the gluten in the dough, developing it to its strength. To *knead* well, you use your hands (your clean hands), your arms and back and legs, but start with your fingers. Dust your hands with flour and work some flour into the dough with your fingertips. Some dough may stick to your fingers, but what do you care? Keep working a little flour in until it is a solid mass, then rub the sticky dough off your fingers with a little flour. Kneading is a practiced motion: push down and away with the heels of both hands, roll it back and push it away again, two or three times until it is wider, then fold it across on itself and turn it to begin again. When it feels sticky, sprinkle it with flour (you may use one or two cups while kneading). Knead the dough for 7 or 10 minutes and roll it up into a ball. It will feel smooth and springy. Pour a little oil into your hands and lightly coat the ball of dough so a dry "skin" won't form while it is rising. Drop it back into its bowl and cover it with a slightly damp dishtowel.

When it has risen for 50 minutes (the dough has risen enough when it holds the dents made by two fingers without springing back) slowly punch it down with your fist, 30 times, and set it to rise under its towel for 40 minutes.

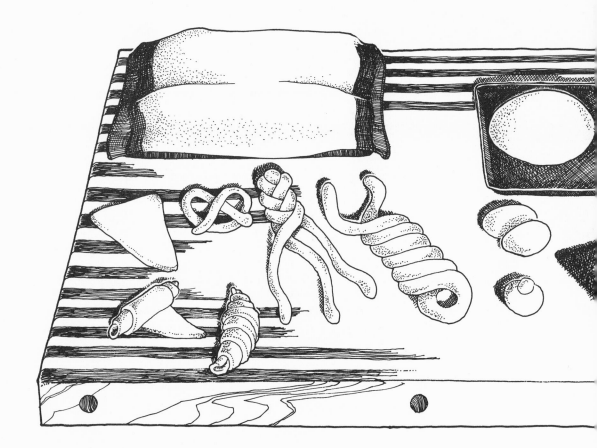

Roll the dough out onto the breadboard (your flat surface) and cut it into two or three pieces. Oil or grease two cookie sheets or any wide, flat oven tins, and dust them lightly with cornmeal.

Now you are ready to make your loaves. Next to deciding when to begin, this is the hardest part of baking bread: what kinds of loaves? Good grief! There are thousands of shapes, more than that. You could make bread every week for years and still discover loaves you hadn't baked, so you

might as well start with something simple and move on from there. Start with round loaves or long loaves. Roll the dough into itself tightly, like rolling up a rug, for long loaves. For round loaves, roll in from the edges all around. Turn the loaf over to put the seam (where the rolling meets) underneath, plump the loaf into shape like a pillow, and set it on the cookie sheet with plenty of room around it. Let each loaf rest under a towel for 30 minutes.

egg
lukewarm water

Preheat your oven to 350° and put the racks toward the middle, but leave room for rising loaves.

Score the top of the loaves with a sharp knife about a quarter of an inch deep to allow them to expand without cracking. Bakers can sign their bread this way, scoring with their own mark. Paint the loaves with a *glaze* mixed up with an egg and a few tablespoons of water. You could sprinkle on sesame seeds or poppy seeds, now, or you could slide the loaves into the hot oven without them.

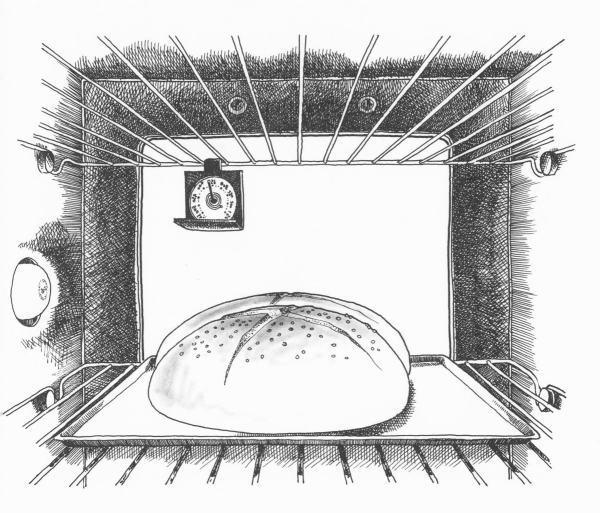

Let the loaves bake for 50 minutes. If they are small loaves or thin loaves or rolls, bake them a shorter time. You can test them by taking them out and thumping their bottoms with a finger: a finished loaf has a deep, hollow sound. You can probe inside with a toothpick or metal rod; an undone loaf will leave sticky bits on the probe. If you are fairly sure, you can cut the loaf open and check. If it is not done, just put it back in for 5 or 10 minutes.

And now you are as lucky as a king. Luckier: you have loaves of rich, real bread you have made yourself and no kingdom to worry about. You can cut your warm loaves (with a serrated knife) and spread the slices with salted butter or sweet (unsalted) butter, with apple butter or peach butter or peanut butter, with cream cheese and strawberry jam, you can toast it and spread it with cottage cheese, you can dip it in soup, you can make sandwiches so good that you aren't sad when all the roast beef or cheese or salami is gone, because you still have a bite of tasty crust left, you can slice it thin and spread it with deviled ham, and of course you can share it.

The Little Red Hen in the story made a big mistake: just because she made her bread alone, she insisted on eating it alone. You *can* eat up your bread by yourself, yes, but it's bitter bread when it's hoarded. If you give some away, the loaf you keep tastes better.

Cool hot bread on cooling racks, and when they are cool, put the loaves you will not use right away in a bread box, or wrap them up, or best, wrap them and chuck them into the freezer. Refrigerating bread will not keep it fresh—only eating it up will.

Once you have baked one loaf you can bake ten, and once you have baked whole-wheat molasses-honey bread, you can bake white bread or bagels or Syrian bread or any kind of bread—the skills are the same, even when the ingredients and timing differ. You should change and experiment on your own after the first half-dozen batches. You should read cookbooks and ask bakers about new breads to bake, and you should bake as often as it feels right. It is basic, simple stuff, but of all the good things you make in your kitchen, nothing will ever taste better than new, warm bread.

HERB BREAD, fragrant and tasty

Make white bread by the basic recipe. When you make loaves, roll them out about one-half inch thick and sprinkle over them: finely diced onions and celery sautéed in butter; thyme, rosemary, and a hint of sage ground in a mortar & pestle; chopped, fresh parsley. Roll the loaf up like a jelly roll and pinch it closed along the bottom. Glaze and bake at 350° for about 50 minutes.

BAGELS, every home should have at least 200 on hand

Sponge: 1½ cups warm water
1 package yeast
¼ cup sugar
3 cups unbleached white flour
(you can add diced onion to the sponge
for onion bagels)
Rise: 60 minutes
Fold in: ½ cup oil
2 teaspoons salt
2-3 cups flour
Knead; Rise, 50 minutes
Punch down; Rise, 20 minutes
Roll dough into a long rope one-inch thick and cut
into five-inch lengths.
Wrap a length around two fingers and roll the ends
together on a floured surface to make
rings of dough.
Drop the rings into boiling water for 30 seconds.
Space the rings on an oiled cookie sheet and glaze,
adding perhaps some poppy or sesame seeds.
Bake 20 to 25 minutes at 425° until golden. Mighty good.

SHIP'S BISCUIT, hard and plain, a standby

Work 2 teaspoons of shortening into 2 cups of flour and a half teaspoon salt with your fingertips. Make a stiff dough with a little less than 1 cup of water. Roll it out on a floured surface to about half an inch thick. Fold it over to six layers and—ready?—beat it with a wooden mallet! Beat it until it's a big pancake again and fold it again. Beat and fold five or six times, then cut the big pancake into circles or squares and bake on a greased sheet at 325° for about 40 minutes, until they just begin to brown their edges.

PITA, Syrian pocket bread

Make a dough of: 2 cups water
2 packages yeast
¼ teaspoon sugar
¼ cup olive oil
1½ tablespoons salt
6 cups hard wheat flour

Knead, 10 minutes

Rise, 90 minutes

Punch down and shape into 8 or 9 balls

Rise, 30 minutes

Roll out balls with a floured rolling pin to one-eighth inch thickness.

Knead lightly and bake on an oiled cookie sheet sprinkled with cornmeal at high heat (500°) on the lowest rack of the oven for 5 minutes, on the highest rack for 3 or 4 minutes or until golden.

The loaves will puff up like soccer balls while baking and deflate while cooling. Wrap them tightly when still slightly warm.

31

CORNBREAD, very quick, smoky and grainy

Slowly fry some bacon, save the bacon grease, and crumble the crisp bacon into a batter you mix from:　1 cup cornmeal

> 1 cup flour
> 1 cup milk
> 1 egg
> ¼ cup sugar
> ½ teaspoon salt
> 4 teaspoons baking powder
> ¼ cup of the bacon grease

Beat your batter 100 times, till it is smooth, and pour it into a greased pan (9 x 12) or greased muffin tins. Bake 25 minutes at 425°.

HARRY DEWEY SCHOOL
7025 Falcon Road
Fair Oaks, CA 95628-4599

641.3   ADKINS   44130
A   BAKERS

5.95